THE
JOHN BUTLER T[
SONGBOOK volume one

GUITAR TAB

JaRRaH

Exclusive Distributors for
Australia & New Zealand:
Music Sales Pty. Limited
120 Rothschild Avenue,
Rosebery NSW 2018, Australia

This book © Copyright 2005
by Wise Publications
ISBN 1 921029 30 7
Order No. MS04090
Printed by McPherson's Printing Group
Design by Glen Hannah @ Goonga Design
Publishing Manager: Melissa Whitelaw
Special thanks to David Weston, Music Sales London
All songs arranged by Martin Shellard, except *Something's Gotta Give* arranged by Arthur Dick
The text pages of this songbook have been printed on 100% recycled paper

Photo credits:
Front and Back Cover - Kim Tonelli
Contents Page - Reinhard Naekel, n-foto@web.de
Page 4 - Kim Tonelli
Page 5 - Tom Walker
Page 6 - Ferne Millen
Page 7 - Mark Grimwade
Page 8 - Ferne Millen

www.johnbutlertrio.com

Wise Publications
part of The Music Sales Group
London/NewYork/Sydney/Paris/Copenhagen/Madrid

CONTENTS

Michael Barker
Drums, Percussion & Backing Vocals

John Butler
Guitar & Vocals

Shannon Birchall
Double Bass, Electric Bass & Backing Vocals

What you want to say,
What till you get home,
I don't want to hear over
the (tele)phone.
But tell how you feel
For I am lonely too
Need you to know
I'm just as scared + numb as you.
Ask me what will be, I don't know
But Balance I will walk through
But I can't show
Ask me what I see, I don't know
But Balance I will walk through
#1
But you've have today.
For which no-one can steal
And it don't matter what I get
or how much it appeals.
For you're always away
And I am stuck @ home
I don't see why I have
to live this life alone.
(c) I hope
there is a way
to make up for old mistakes.
I know
What happening.
for a good reason.

BETTERMAN....

I am since I come, I come into contact with
you. And you taught me so many things about myself
and you know this is True.

But know we are apart and it's all my fault
cause you know I need to be alone. Don't Know
myself so how can I share me with you girl or anyone.

Don't want be a thorn in your side Good Woman. Always be
the one to make you cry, don't want to that guy good
woman. Cause you deserve everything and I get nothing so
leave me. And I'll go away better off I stay far from you.
Cause you are Beautiful.

Typical man I am cause you think I want my cake and
eat it too. Cause say I can't be in a relationship but I still
feel for you. Cause you are the best woman this old man
have ever met, you taught me about my Soul, you shared
with me your Magic.

Don't want to be thorn in your side Good Woman. Always be the
one to make you cry, don't want to be that guy Good Woman.
Cause you deserve everything and I get nothing so leave me. And
I'll go away better off I stay far from You. Cause you are
Beautiful. ● Beautiful Woman....

Better Man

Words & Music by John Butler

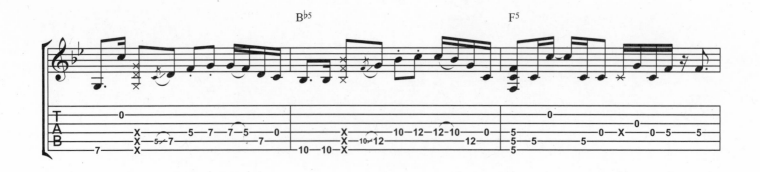

1. So bet - ter - man, I am since I
man, I am be - cause you

think come in - to con - tact with you. And
I want my cake, and eat it too. 'Cause say

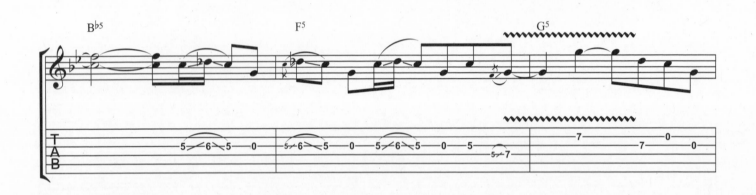

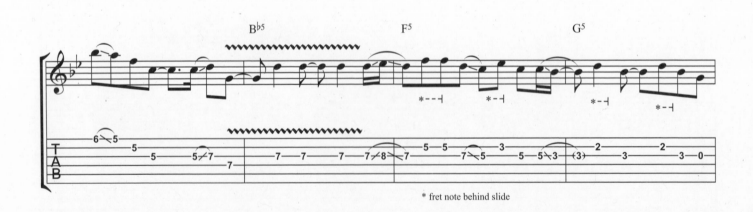

* fret note behind slide

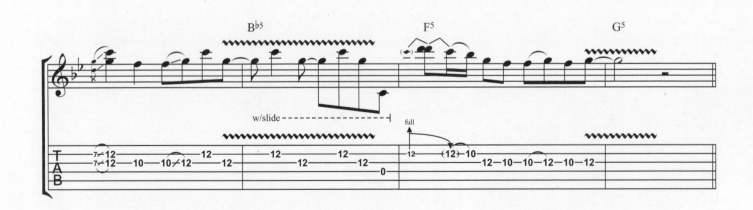

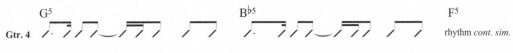

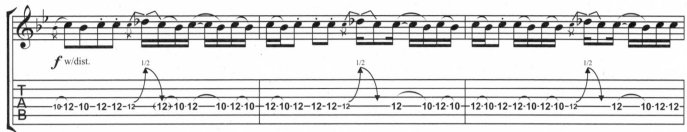

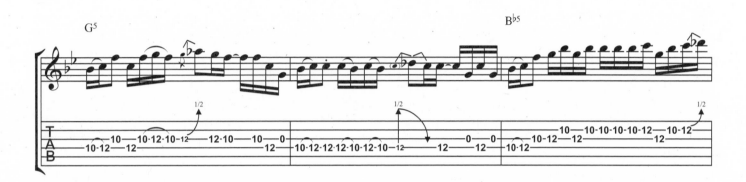

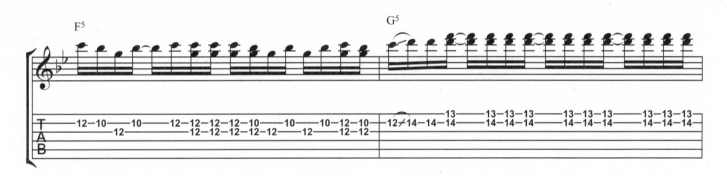

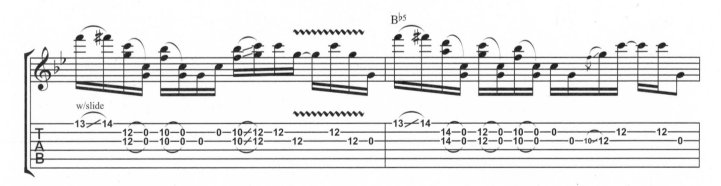

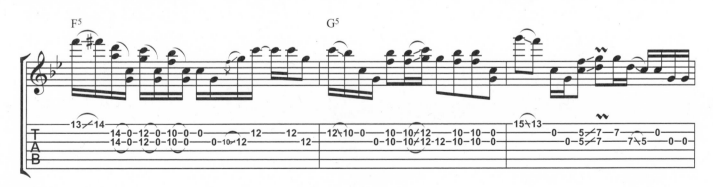

*fret strings in front of slide

Interlude

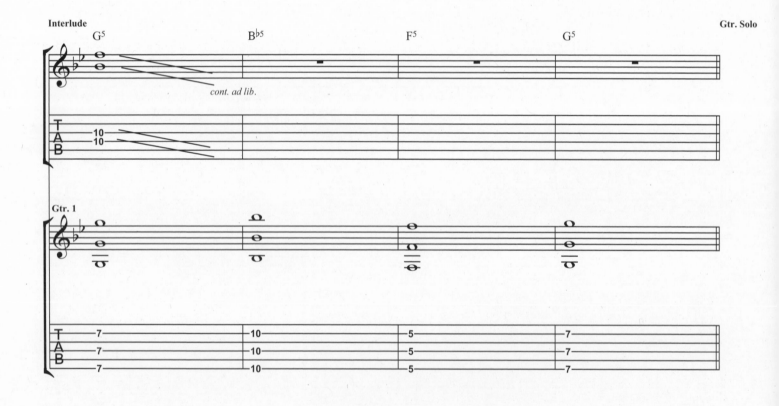

Gtr. Solo

cont. ad lib.

Gtr. 1

Bass solo

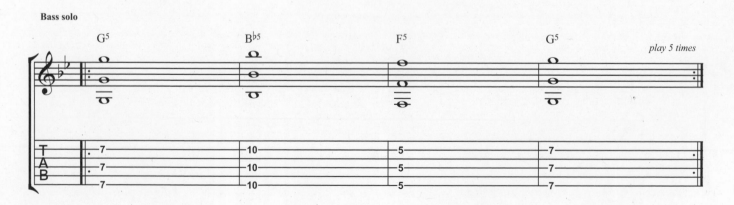

play 5 times

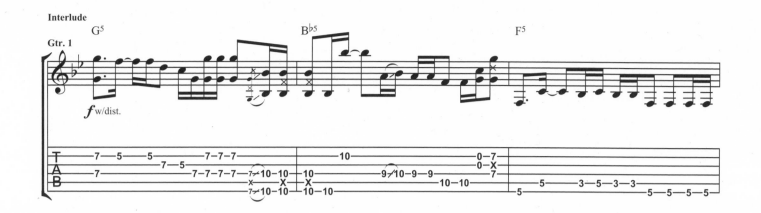

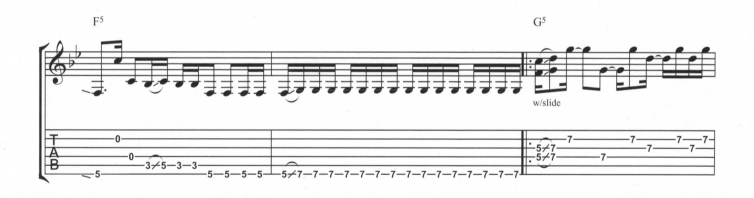

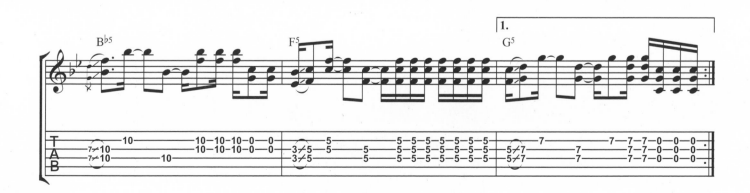

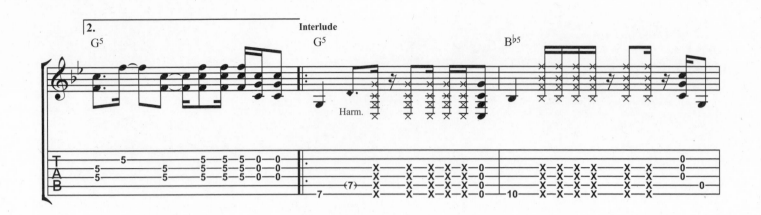

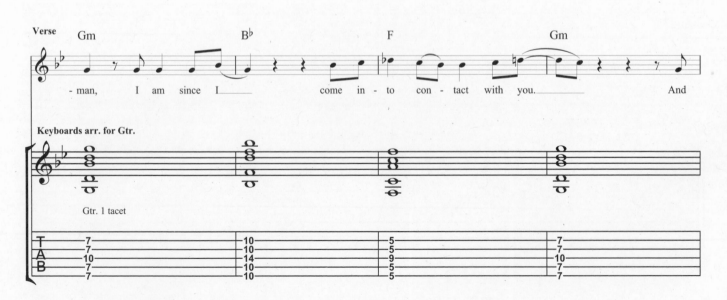

Hello

Words & Music by John Butler

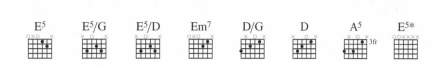

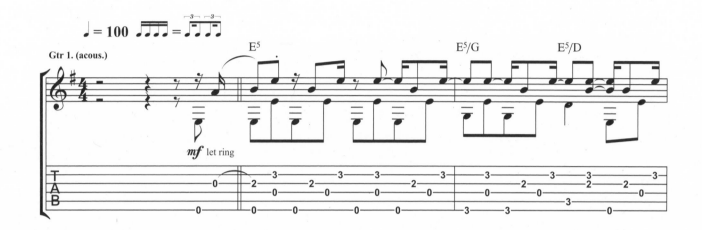

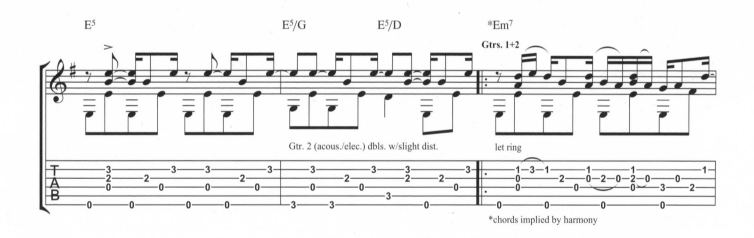

Gtr. 2 (acous./elec.) dbls. w/slight dist.

*chords implied by harmony

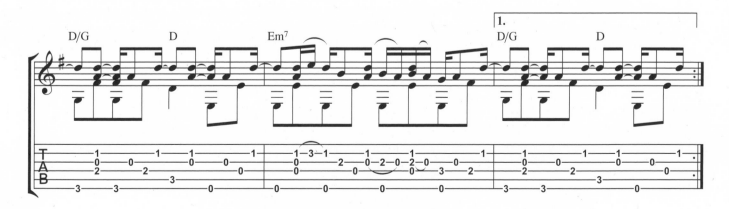

25

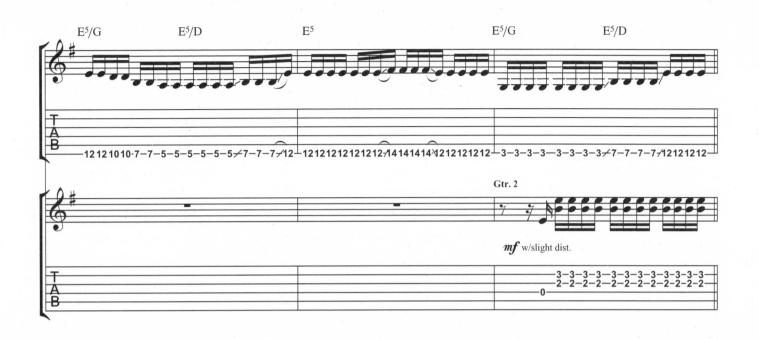

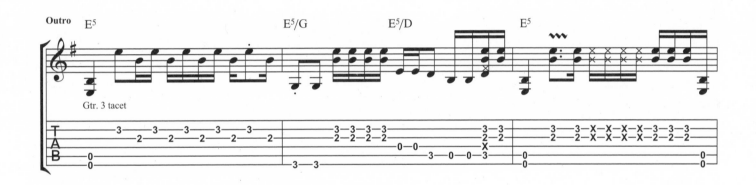

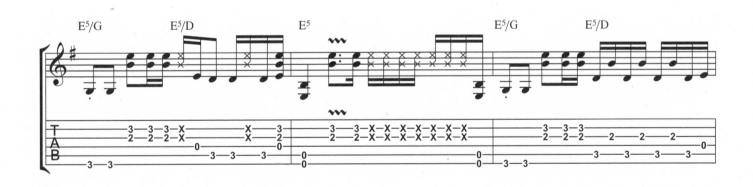

Home Is Where The Heart Is

Words & Music by John Butler

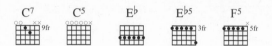

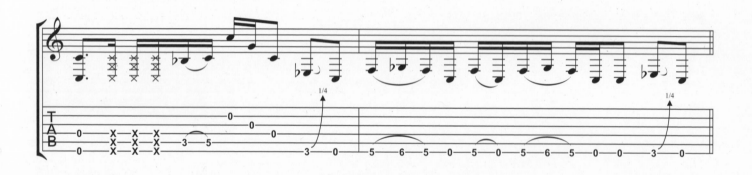

home   is   where   the   heart ____ is   yeah, _____   home.

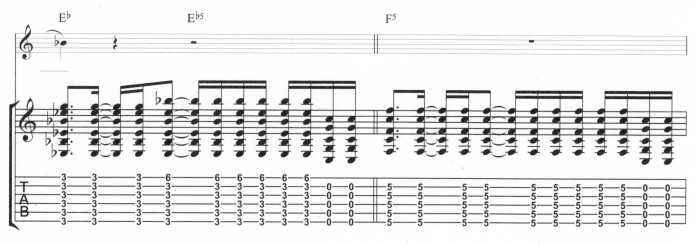

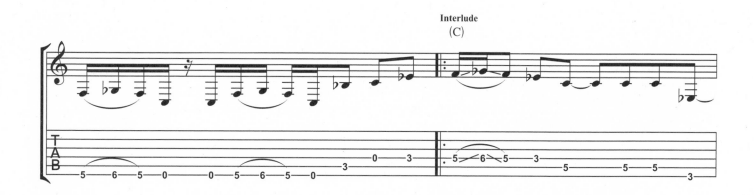

Interlude
(C)

1.

Interlude

C⁵

And

Verse

(C)

then they got the nerve to say, they be tak-ing our jobs a-way. Ev-en though half the jobs that we're work-ing for man, are owned

Bass arr. for gtr.

from the ov-er-seas. And the oth-er half of the com-pan-ies, yes, yes, that they say that we right-ly own. They

op-er-ate on aisle three, third world. That's right___ yeah, the sweat-shop zone. And I___ say.

I don't know whats go - ing on.___ Don't___ know what the hell to say.
I don't know what's go - ing on.___ Don't___ know the rea - son why.

The gov - ern - ment___ de - cides on let - ting
We live in a___ e - du - cat - ed, do - called

re - fu - gees___ in and when they get here yes, they are de - tained.___ And
de - mo - cra - cy.___ Where eve - ry - bo - dy de - cides to be-

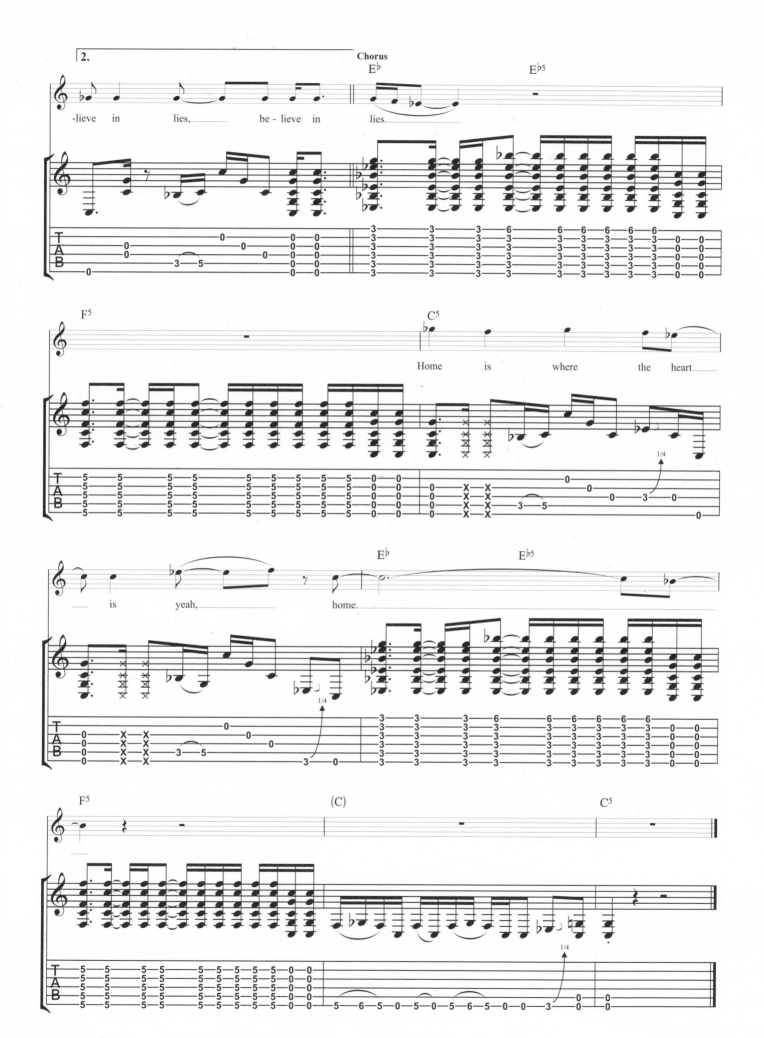

Pickapart

Words & Music by John Butler

* Tap and hold chord w/picking hand
left hand plays legato

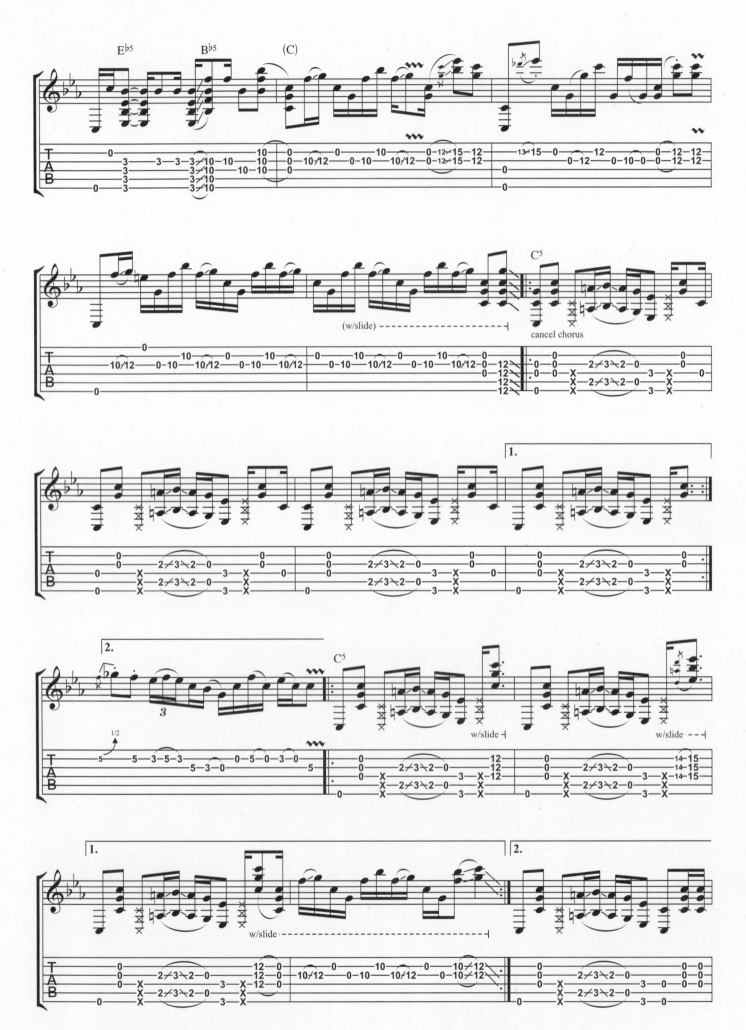

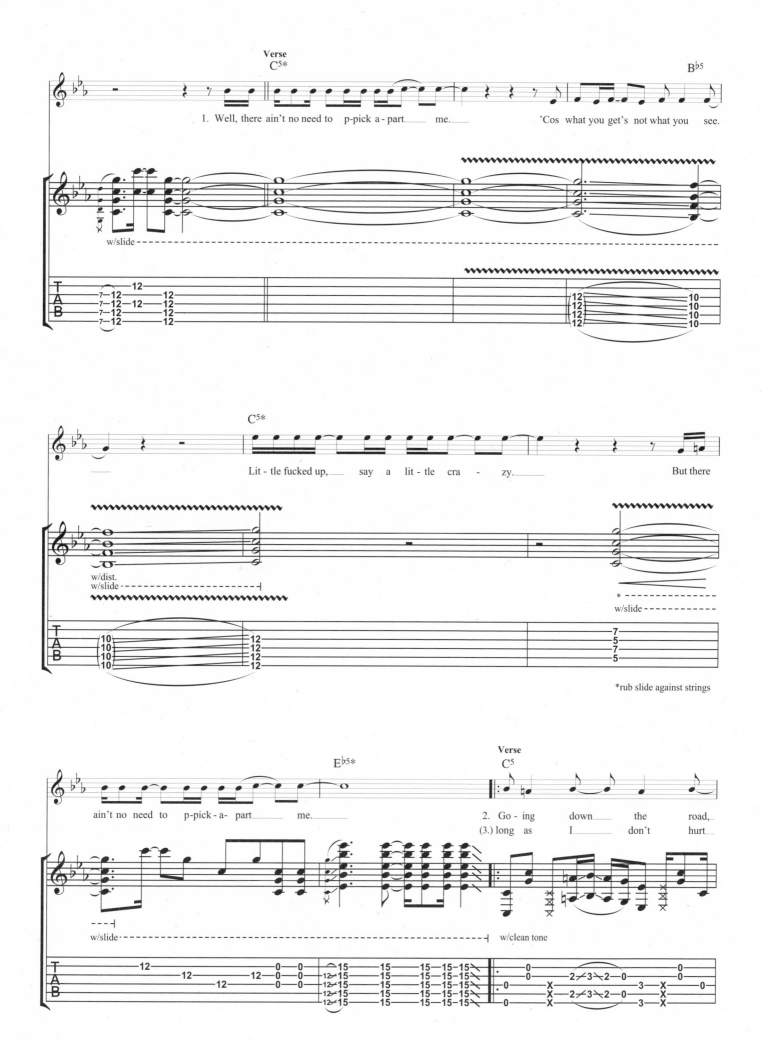

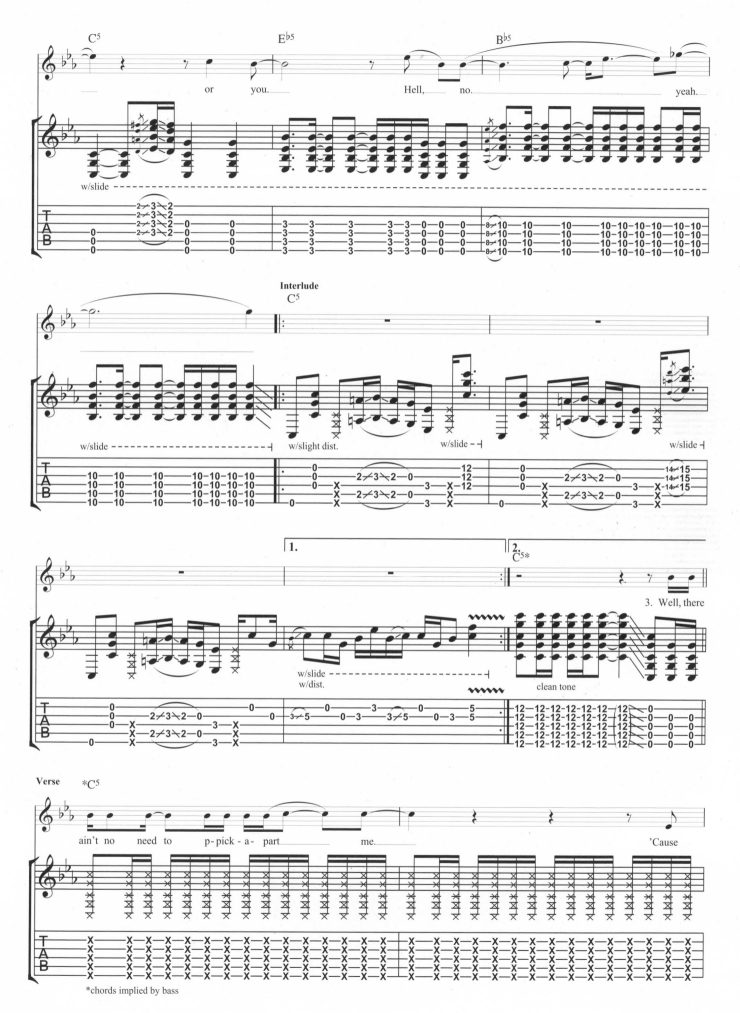

41

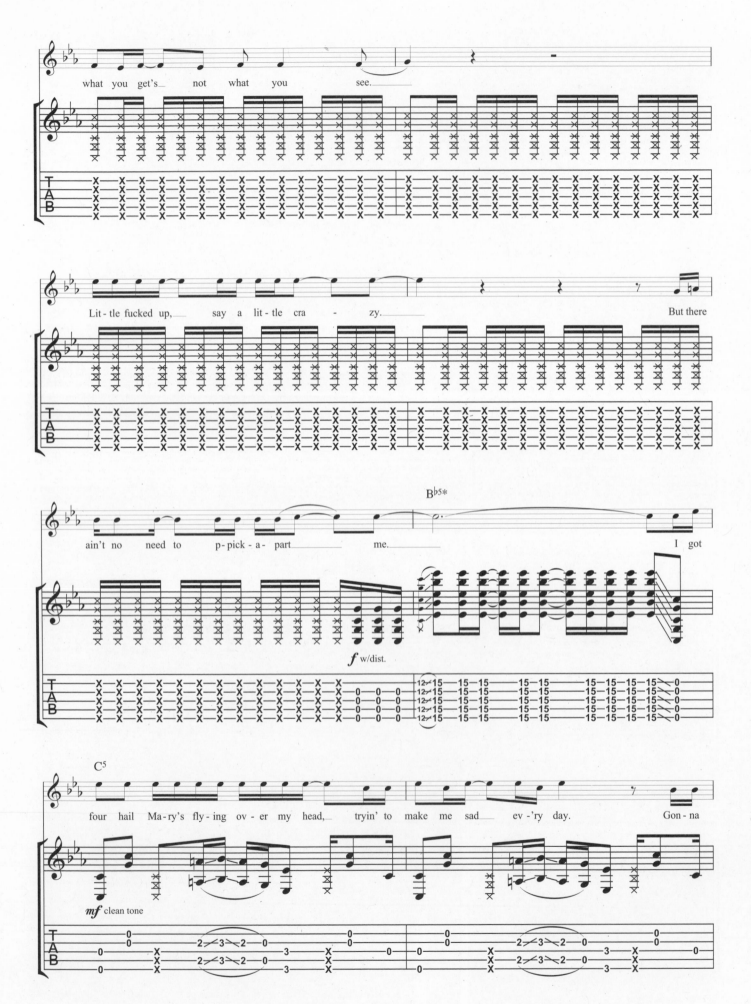

what you get's___ not what you see.___

Lit - tle fucked up,___ say a lit - tle cra - zy.___ But there

ain't no need to p- pick - a - part___ me.___ I got

four hail Ma - ry's fly - ing ov - er my head,___ tryin' to make me sad___ ev -'ry day. Gon - na

shoot me those lit - tle moth-er-fuck-ers down__ with my po - si - tive ar - til - le - ry.__ 'Cos it

does - n't rea - lly mat - ter who you lis - ten to, or who yeah, you gon - na be - lieve.__ I said

*C5

no-thing real - ly stop-ping me or an - y - bo - dy else from go - ing and a - be - ing__ free.

*chords implied by bass

Gtr. solo C5

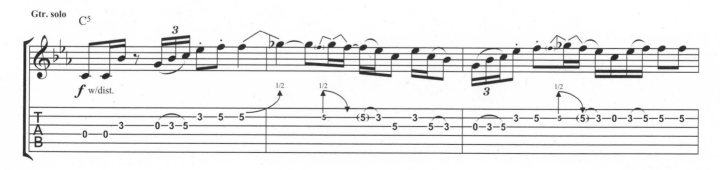

43

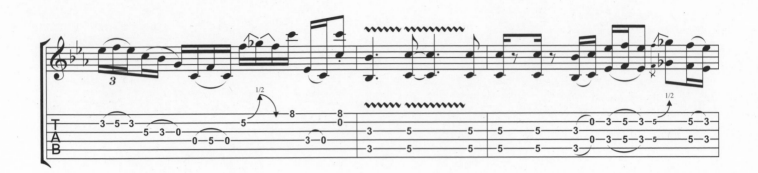

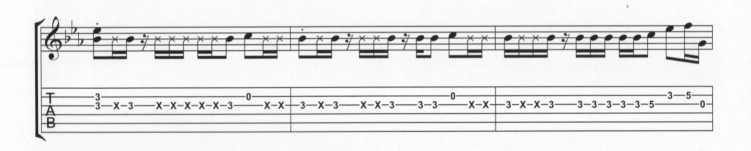

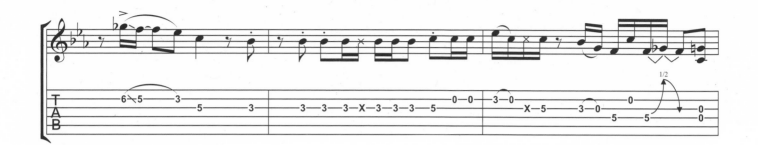

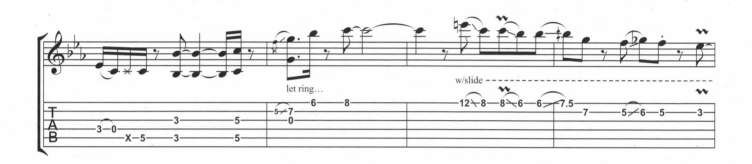

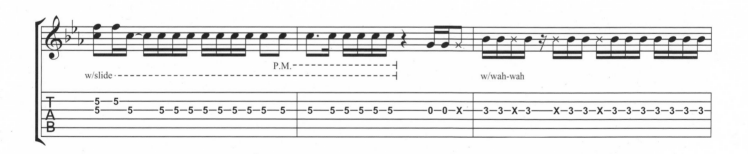

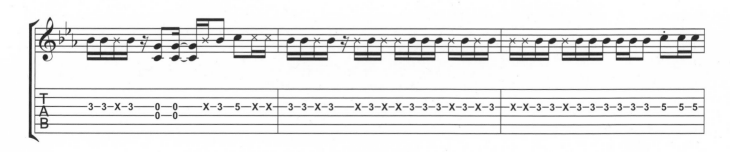

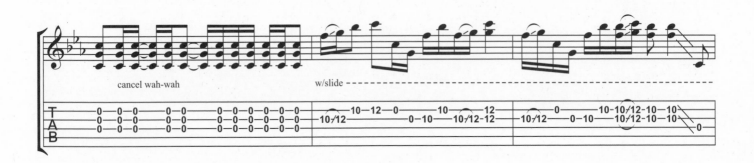

cancel wah-wah

w/slide -

w/slide -

w/slide -

Interlude

C⁷

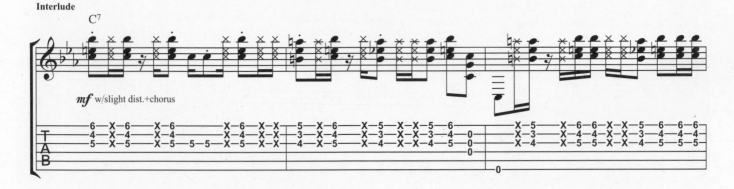

mf w/slight dist.+chorus

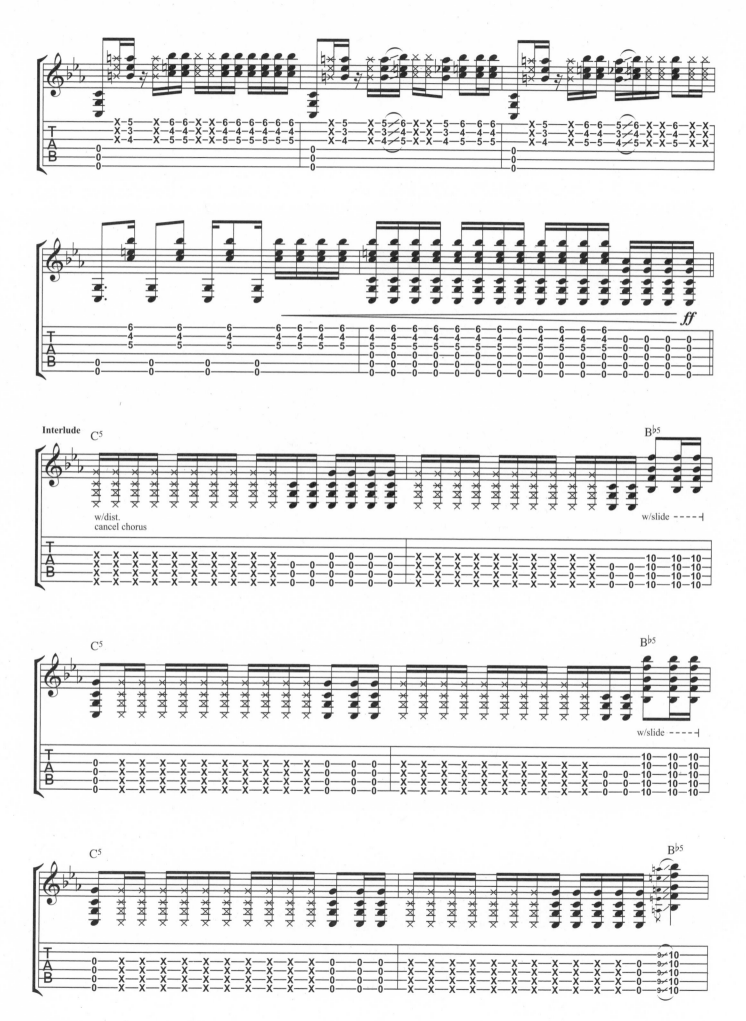

48

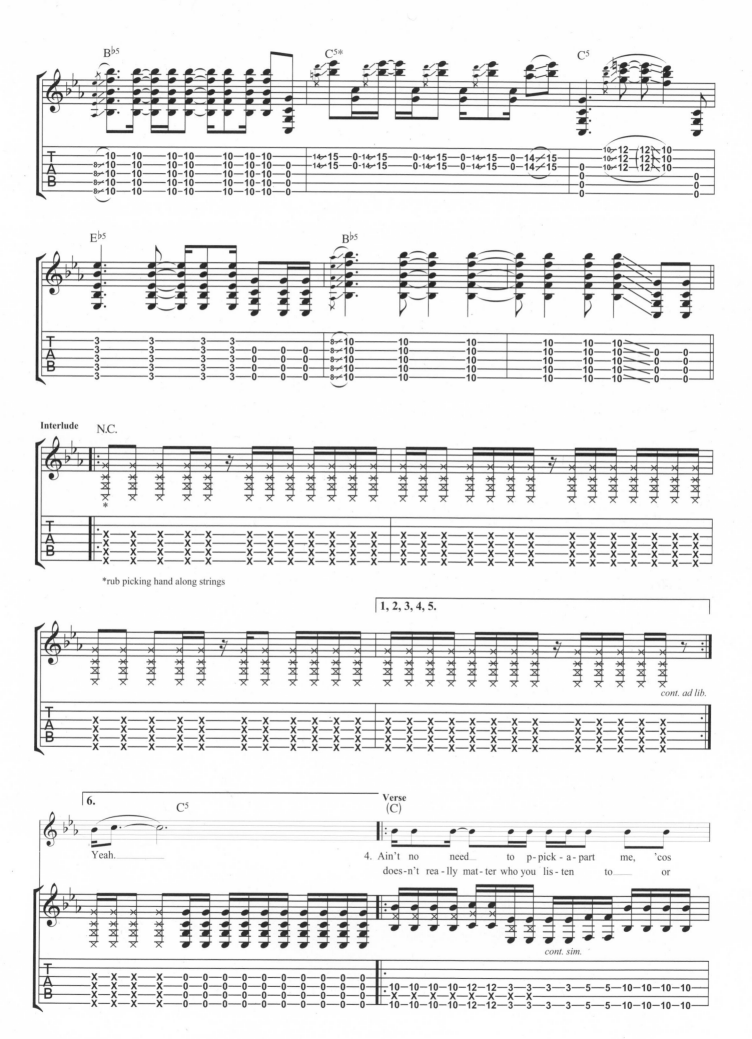

*rub picking hand along strings

1, 2, 3, 4, 5.

cont. ad lib.

6.

Yeah.

Verse
(C)

4. Ain't no need   to p-pick - a- part   me, 'cos
doesn't really mat-ter who you lis-ten to   or

cont. sim.

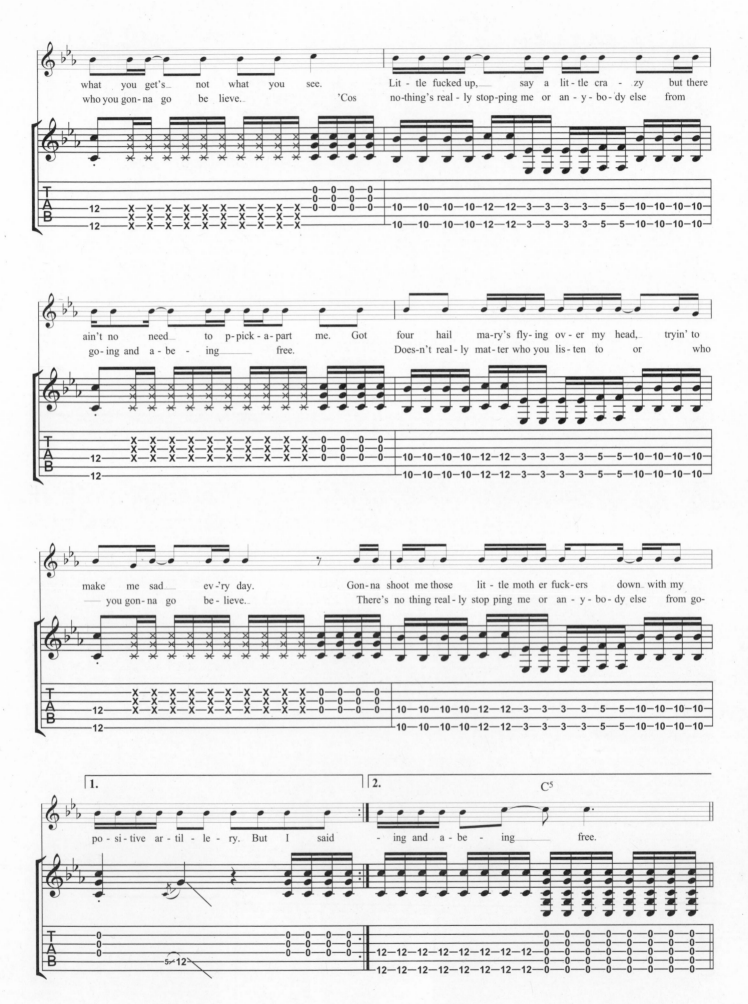

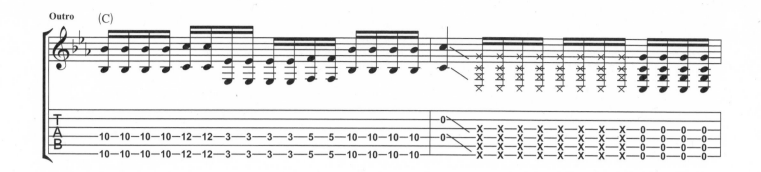

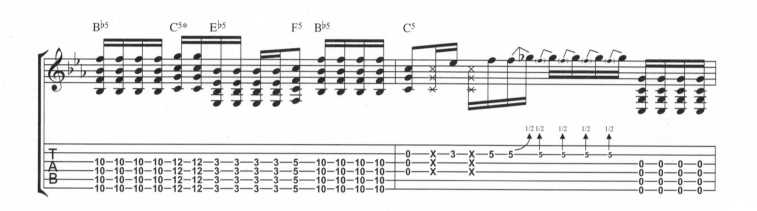

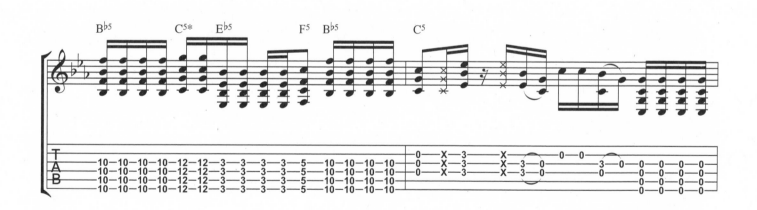

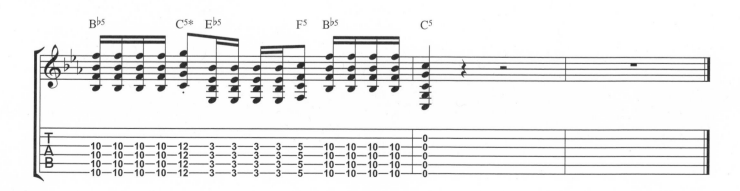

Something's Gotta Give

Words & Music by John Butler

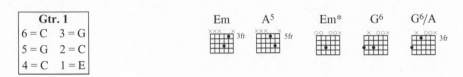

think a-bout these cats run-nin' the world with hate. I say,
leak-ing so much, now man, it's burn-in' my eyes, yeah. Can't you just
head-lines read-ing, "God bless the U. S. A." and I thought,
drive and pray all day to the guy a-bove. But e-ven-tu-a-lly the on-ly gua-ran-

some-thing's got to give. Got the
throw that damn pot out. And on the
God bless ev-'ry-one. God bless the
-tee will be that the tea in your tank will run dry. Be-cause

1° Gtr. 2 (elec.) w/wah ad lib. ad lib. fill

cont. sim.

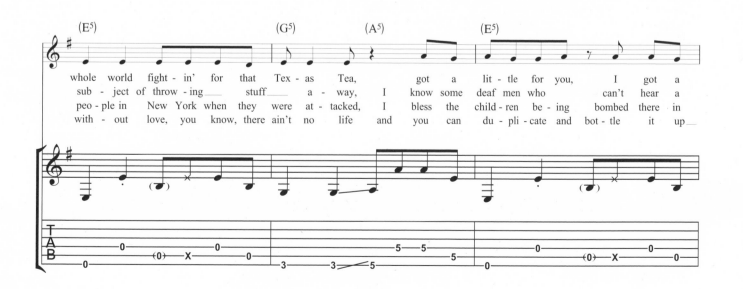

whole world fight-in' for that Tex-as Tea, got a lit-tle for you, I got a
sub-ject of throw-ing stuff a-way, I know some deaf men who can't hear a
peo-ple in New York when they were at-tacked, I bless the child-ren be-ing bombed there in
with-out love, you know, there ain't no life and you can du-pli-cate and bot-tle it up

53

I get an-oth-er try, boy.

open out…

Chorus

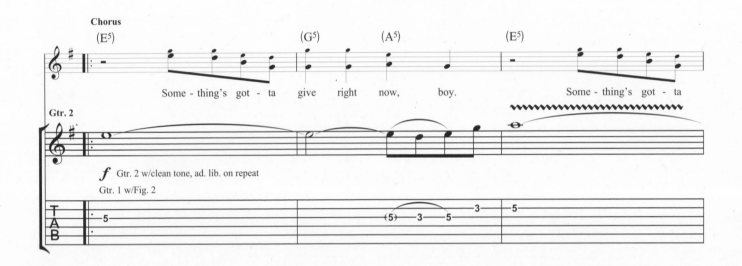

Some - thing's got - ta give right now, boy. Some - thing's got - ta

Gtr. 2

f Gtr. 2 w/clean tone, ad. lib. on repeat
Gtr. 1 w/Fig. 2

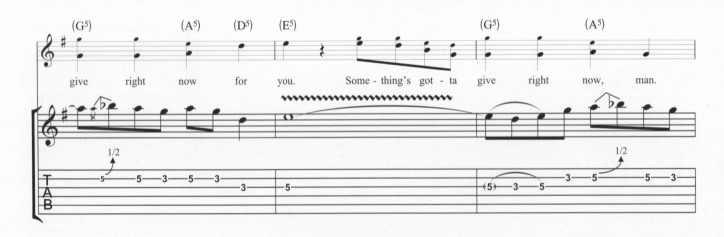

give right now for you. Some - thing's got - ta give right now, man.

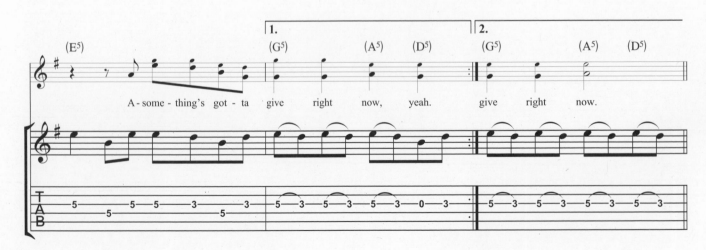

A - some - thing's got - ta give right now, yeah. give right now.

56

Treat Yo Mama

Words & Music by John Butler

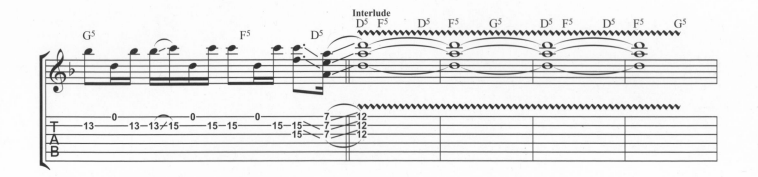

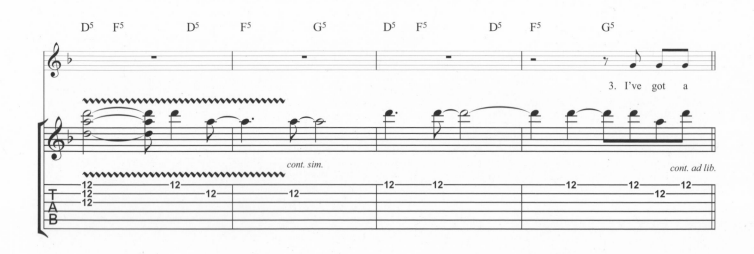

3. I've got a

cou - ple of friends up in a tree in North - Cliff. You know they're do - ing their part, you know they're

do - ing their bit. Try - ing to save our moth - er from all this greed. You know they

- po - rate greed.

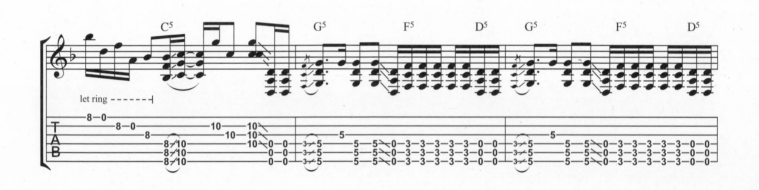

let ring - - - - - -┤

What You Want

Words & Music by John Butler

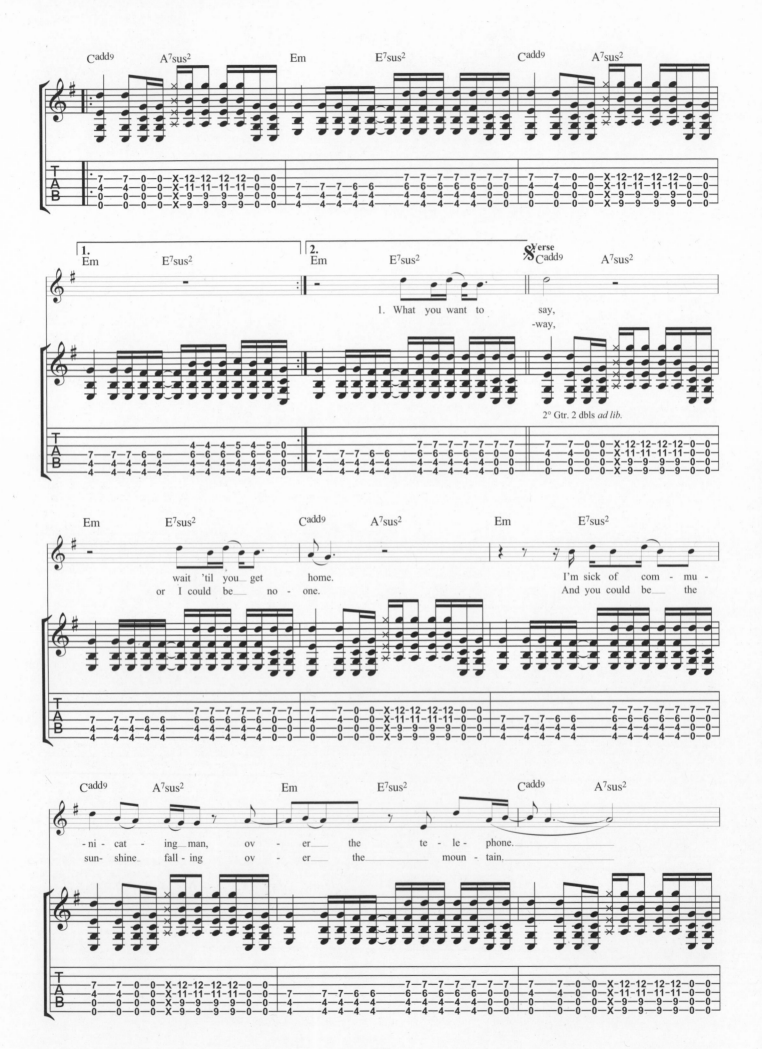

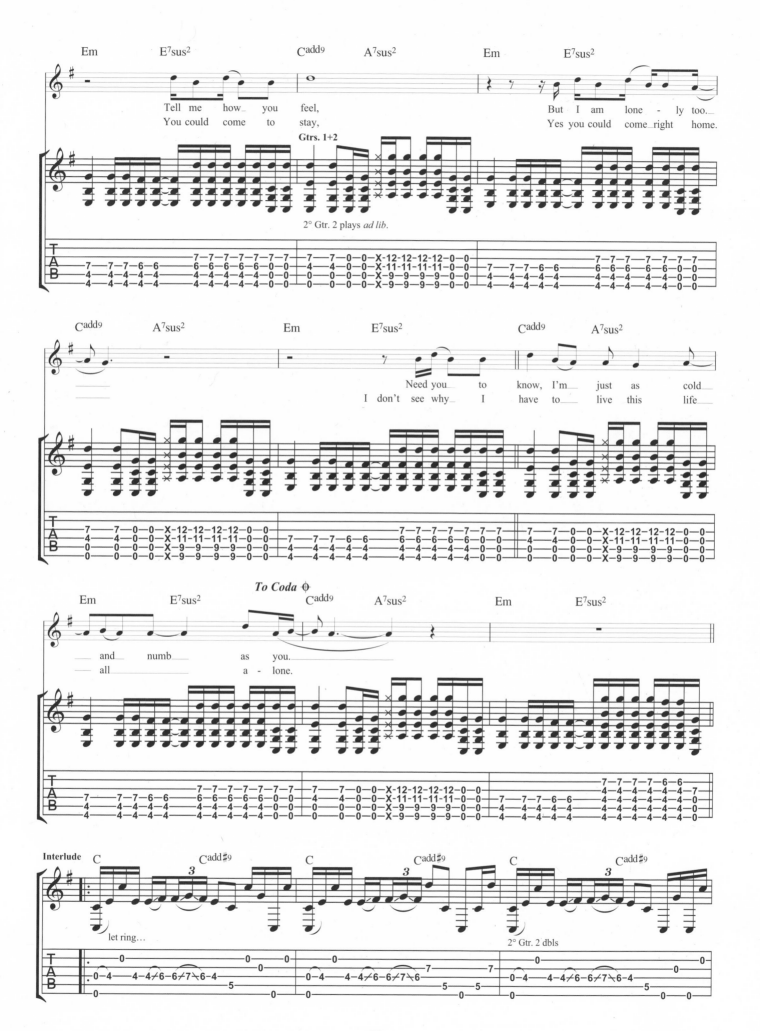

69

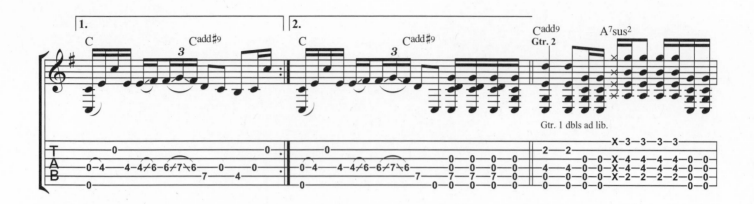

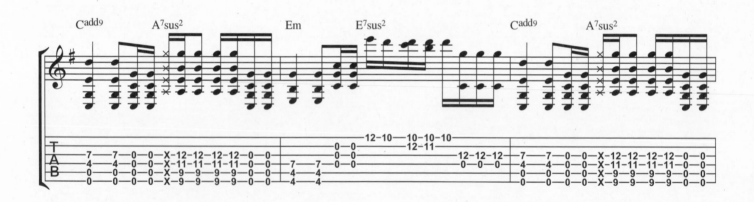

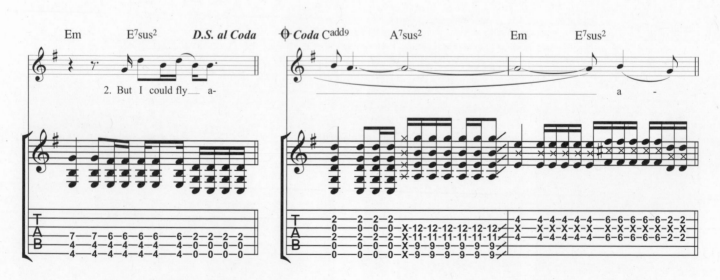

2. But I could fly a-

a -

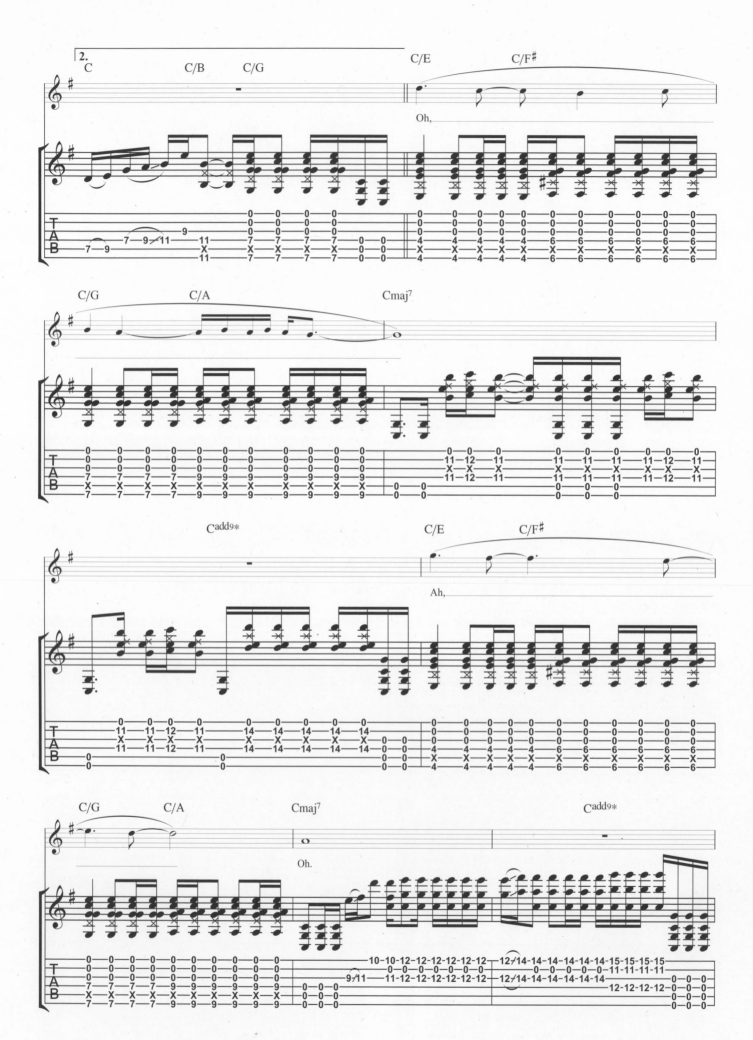

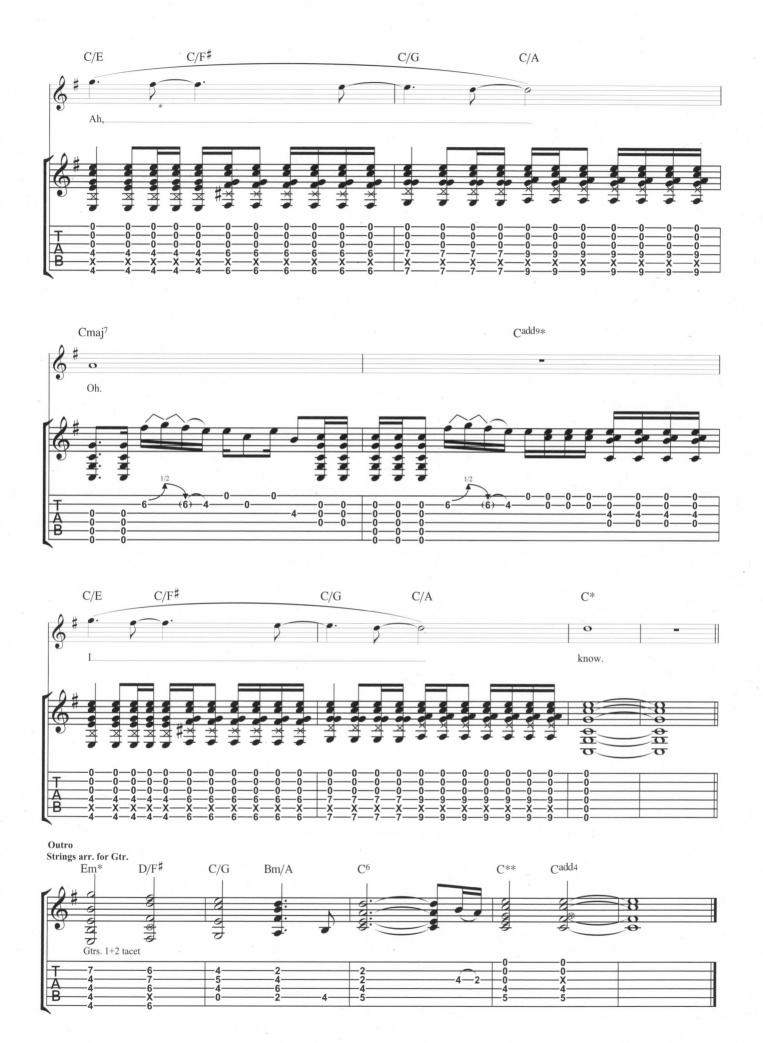

Zebra

Words & Music by John Butler

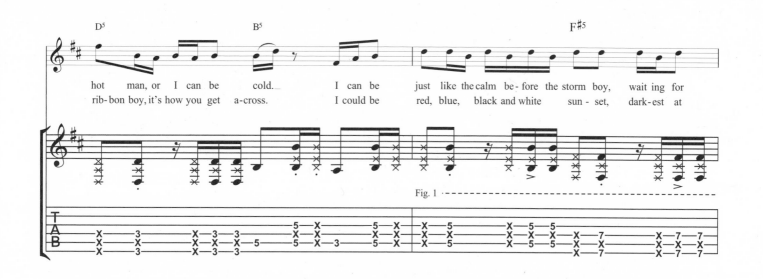

La, da, da, da, da. Hell___ who know?___ Da - da, da - da,

la, da, da, da, da. Hell, who knows? Hell, who knows.___

D⁵ B⁵

F♯5 D⁵ B⁵ D⁵ B⁵

1. **2.**

2. I could be

Gtr. Solo B⁵ F♯5 D⁵ B⁵ F♯5 D⁵ B⁵

w/slide -
w/dist.+wah-wah

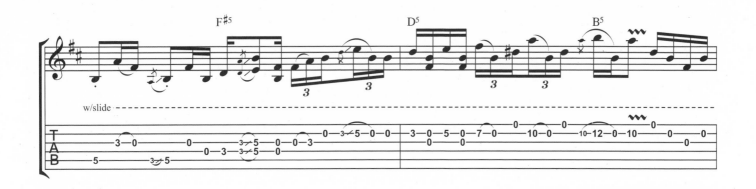

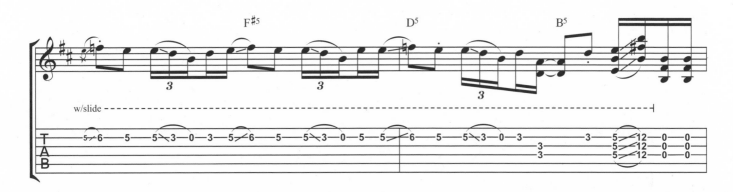

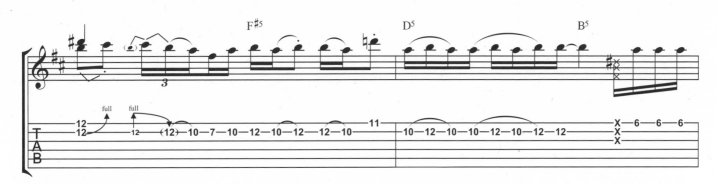

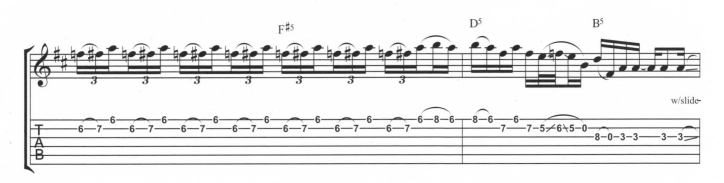

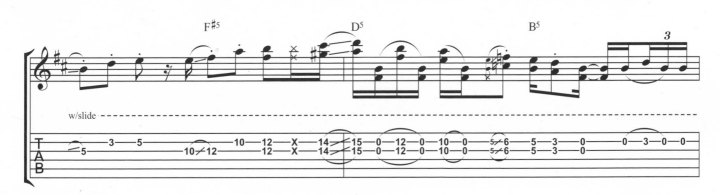

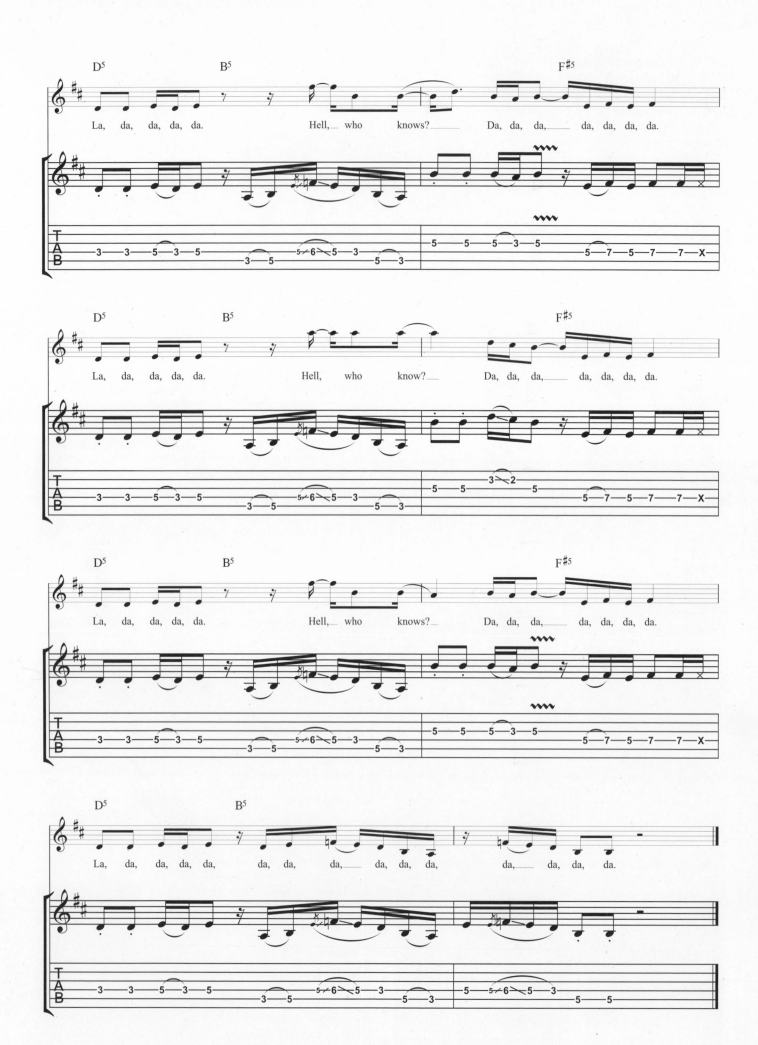